Abracadabra

2006

Abracadabra

poems by Kimberly Lyons

Granary Books
New York City 2000

ISBN 1-887123-31-8

Printed in the United States of America
on acid free paper in an edition of 1000

Cover image by Tony Fitzpatrick

Book design by Emily Y. Ho

Granary Books, Inc.
307 Seventh Avenue, Suite 1401
New York, NY 10001 USA

info@granarybooks.com
http://www.granarybooks.com

for Mitch & Jackson

Accumulation.
Love,
degeneration,...
and regenerated dives

    —Joseph Ceravolo

Acknowledgements & Notification

Some of the work in this book previously appeared in the following publications: *An Anthology of New (American) Poets, Cuz, The Gertrude Stein Awards in Innovative American Poetry: 1993-1994, The Hat, Lingo, Long News in the Short Century, Mass. Ave, New American Writing, Pagan Place, The Poetry Project Newsletter, Red Weather, West Coast Line, o.blek*, and *The World*. Thanks very much to the editors.

To the poets and friends who came to the Poetry Project, the Ear Inn, Biblios, Zinc Bar, and Teachers & Writers, many thanks for listening all these years. I am particularly grateful to Steve Clay, Julie Harrison, Joe Eliot, and Anne Noonan for their many acts of kindness. Thank you, Tony Fitzpatrick.

The organization of this book is circular. *Details & Incidents* comprises a selection from most recent work (up to 1999). Many thanks to Laurie Price for the B-day collage titled *Draft*.While Chez Es Saada might be seen on First Street, Café Silverio belonged to Lorca's hero, Silverio Franconetti, who's mentioned in Lorca's *Flamenco Vignettes*. Daina Lyons brought to my attention the lovely, odd drawings of one Cecilie Poe–found as a discarded drawing pad in a Chi town Goodwill.

The second section, *Abracadabra*, brings together a selection from a set of poems written in 1996-1997. Vyt Bakaitis–much appreciation for the postcard from Madrid that led to this piece. "Turn" refers to the publication of part of a long poem by Mitch Highfill (Situations, 1997).

One Hundred Famous Views of Edo (titled, obviously, after the famous Hiroshige prints) contains selected poems from 1981-1991. Nick Dorsky's wonderful film *17 Reasons Why* inspired–like, right after I got home–"Aphra."

Object Relations is a selection of works from 1991-1996. "Eon" was written specifically for the Poetry Project's group reading at the 1996 symposium on content. LAB–thanks for the encouragement to notify. *K.L.*

Contents

Details & Incidents
Chez Es Saada *11*
Draft *14*
Dandelion *15*
Neptune Avenue *16*
Details & Incidents *17*
Cafe Silverio *19*
Biscotti *22*
For Cecilie Poe *24*
Side Shows by the Seashore *26*

Abracadabra
Peony *31*
Attachment *32*
The Concise History of Painting *33*
Series *34*
My Cookbooks *35*
Go Dog Go *36*
Madrid *38*
After "Turn" *39*
Abracadabra *40*

One Hundred Famous Views of Edo
Tectonic *43*
Duration *44*
Shower *53*
Looking for Mina Loy *54*
Ma Griffe *55*
Bright Blue *56*
Rayographs *58*
A Fragment of A *59*
Aphra *60*
One Hundred Famous Views of Edo *64*

Object Relations
Object Relations *71*
August *72*
Central Park West *74*
depressed segment of earth *75*
The Hidden Staircase *76*
Jeweled Fifties Bee *77*
The Reginald Marsh Rose Couch With Leopard Trim *78*
Kind *79*
Moon, the Harshest Critic *80*
Vampyr *81*
The Teacup Club *83*
'Tude *84*
Oreos & Cheerios *86*
March 6 *89*
April *90*
Ask Ivanna *91*
Eon *93*

Details
& Incidents

Chez Es Saada

Where is this place.
But that's a sucker's question.
I mean really
is it better to improve and
improve at a defined game
or to fuck-up
in continuous instances
in a situation only possibly
a game

that broadens out
until
as you grimace in fun
at the so-called players
and realize by dint
of their unpremeditated
responses they are in actuality

not "playing"
"that game"
but doing "something else"

And you did state
unequivocally that
there's so many places
just like this one

in fact, such
locations are invented
in a weekend.

In an intractable desert

roses in their cistern
by the wall

joyously perfume the air
with artificiality.

Perforated lanterns.

Memories collide

of this and that

and no one is able to
fully complete the other.

Billy, I think it was,
produced an egg from
his coat and fork
from his hair.

And Susan poured an absinthe.

To undulate our arms in the Arabian style

as all of language clicks
into nested beads.

I don't want to
mess your hair up

said "the driver"

with the wind

something colder than it was

that drags in the
present moment

as though it were a
vintage mirror

nailed to the cement

a sensation
of the body
that

holds the picture to the air.

Draft

Orion, fences and writing
at
peripheries

that hieroglyphic and accumulate

on every strip of distance

I only saw architecturally
blood dips and flame sprouts
their astronomy
horizon's compass and wheat.

To balance thought on the head
a wick, fuel.
Camel's hump.
Collect jars along its curve.
Draft, *work in progress*
the sun says to the old things.

Dandelion

for Tony Fitzpatrick

twin nuclear hands lit the match
dandelion universe in quadrant
puff boils up the hydrogen
red cardinal. Peaked on ledge
air makes with radio waves.
Radiating diagram, the igloo
harmony
and other little scratches ink made
is this powwow gestured scribble
tendrils of the prophecy. That
paper folded on a thought
collides with the century.

Neptune Avenue

A scribbling counterfeit of
white animal on black.

Strip mall procession, the laundry

building, red as a tongue.

Deciduous tentacles

and other trees with
arms.

The Russian complexities
find a signal

rest here in the passage.

The arc of a cyclone
permanently storming across

its pale blue cousin

the sky
with words:

"no admittance."

Details & Incidents

It's cords of appliances that thwart
casual obfuscation of objects.
Wet forgotten laundry
& the old shed out back
where the documents are kept.
Receipts in caved-in boxes
unravels its content
as the night sheds minutes
until like a bone
bereft of the meat
our bed's surface
becomes a skating rink,
a white pail.
I slip into something more sky.
The mauve intangibility of
disturbances on the street
the fringy appearance
of old celery lost in the crisper

emotive random red bird thistle

I thought the dawn returns to you

its lava

and then pour perfect coffee

into an ugly pink & gray Montefiore Hospital mug

and Jackson says look at the bird on the fire escape

its slender iridescent throat, speckled,

strands in beak

its proximity

17 hours later is remembered

among other details and incidents.

Cafe Silverio

Dry as a slipper of
amaranth

the ground
could be the
roof
of an inordinate mouth.

Stems tweaked
antennas provoked
the static interrupts static.

The expository cadence
of seasons
melds to other graphic musics.

It felt vertiginous as I looked
forward into the tunnel the trees
made all of the sky
permeable
as the glassine liquid
of an eye.

The enormous white papers
turn
as one knits classically
obdurate particles into a sweater
the giantess wore swearing
as she drove her calamitous
boots to the
river bed.

It was dry there too, stubbed
with our
vocables. More than is bracketed
by any one day
the hydrangea changes and changes.
Today is burnt as blood,
crisped on the cement.

He lifts his miniature tambourine

and the two young boys clasped.

A signal to
a future, its narrow
black voice radiates
mauve spires.

Like when Mickey Mouse
tickles Donald Duck's
foot, the bed collapses
and they fall together
through a series of
contraptions
to the table where the
rickety sun

bumps along as they eat
twin eggs.

Yakety-yak
everyone says. I heard
this from my
sled.

from
distances
we touch
angles
of each other.
A choreographer's
instructions

Yield
Facet.

The arithmetic
of siren, chimes and
drone

the lavender sphere

bisected by
gold and black words.

Biscotti

Out of the dark tent-like space

abrupt disclosure of

light.

Coffee, leaves,
the sky
seems all particles
and coldly billowing.

The stadium filled with rain.

His feet, curled like snails,
under a sheet.

hard biscotti
surfaces
resist.

I want to be
enveloped by you I tell
him. *Empathize.*

A condition rather than
motion.

spiraled deeper

patches, duration.
Rather than continuity,
spheres, cycles.

I try to write it at a slant.
Now, not even located.

Arm to board, its watery
page.

Grimaces behind her hair.

It ain't moving.

Fired up.

Paler and paler, the
essential object

rid of its oils,

lucky skeleton rides.

For Cecilie Poe

In this new realm

a trapezoidal path

configured of minty chalk and breath.

The leaves race upward.

Our bedroom curtains of lace & flies

describes an astronomy

visible from the farmlands.

The whole sky spills

to approximate these tender drawings.

A life collects from objects, instills

its philology in cerulean tones, evades

the teacher's corrections

and manifests its scenes as a sort of

1950's Greek

theater. The

frosty beam of evening,

a vault of feeling

encases our tango.

Tissue

broken

sprays outward

in blue tints

of early night, a throne

to draw toward you

its powers.

Side Shows by the Seashore

As the train blew in
white rectangles
came from my bag.
A pouch
bitten through
to the
limits.

The blueness of
wooden
transformative hands
zigzag from
the saintly prow.

Orange formica chairs
and slices of
gum sweeten.

the dusted erect
morning. The replica
of its landscape

"wet paint"

It used to come in on
choppy, introverted bits

to be assembled in a
quixotic yet magnetized way.

The vertical slats
of the station's
surfaces

and myriad inscribed
monuments

experienced as partial
signals, pulses

casts the
writer as passive

and the station as a languorous
workshop

along the path of
its arrivals.

A wave of handwriting

smeared on the walls

an orange translucency

twists in its meaty
head.

The puffed white facets
of an enormous room.

I ride in my chair,
try to converge at
the union
of the ecstatic
variations

that resist the human
experimentations upon
their entrances.

We travel, simultaneously,
to our destination

side shows by the seashore.

Abracadabra

Peony

for Martha & Basil King

How such a tightly wound ball
could two days later
extend extravagantly.
Wide as baby's palm (wider)
on a wooden table.
Old musique's
formations of
interpretation.
Consider "home"
vestiges of a
location
outside
any diameter.

Attachment

To take, literally, incidents
slight in themselves
would leave all that nothing.

The word *obliteration* like
a rip in lace
dry November leaves under your shoes
and the ones that will not tear
red as a big teardrop
the flick of fire slowed
to a singular frame
all this the hunter of ice
brought from his belt with his hands.
His three ageless sisters, a trio of voices,
urge him to run
through the sky
after constellations of desire and
resistance,
object and void.

The Concise History of Painting

The cones and cubes of an ideal town
rise across the lake
of brown rumpled water
perfumed by egrets
and moths. And I fell asleep
briefly yesterday by the file cabinet
and had a dream, like a spasm.
Masses of clouds move sternly over
the ocean.
I suck on my violet duck.
I hit my spoon with the floor.
Call out to the
shadow of a saint
who has fallen under his horse.

Series

The saints in Iran, oblique geometries
shapes
are saturated and white
aspirin dust
is on the surfaces

some lines in a cauldron
reappear as polished chrome
of Saturday in November
when the scattered appliances
in apertures gather light to a point

my sense of time is really getting
flabby

now the earth is dry patchy and fog occurs

and milk in a miniature cup

I have no more energy for process

and someone is dragging bells
through the rain.

My Cookbooks

Instruct in the verities
as subjective consciousness
is the hunger of the writer
and the objective correlative,
the recipe.
More gratifying, almost,
than cooked flesh
is the formula
from ancient mothers.
Mme. Ada Boni, editor of Italy's
"leading women's magazine," *Prezoia*
channels:
LARGE EEL, MARINATED
(place eel, like a doughnut in the bottom of pan)
it begins.

Go Dog Go

Blinds
slice the sky
into
levels of
autumnal energy

There's your ball!
A lime green spot
on the floor that covers
my nose
in fluffs, specks, wipes
intangible because of exhaustion
all too evident
(because of exhaustion)
the navy and white stripes
of the atmosphere
order me to
document this mess!

The heavens, more than
liminal excess, display
cavorting poets, darkish cafes,
configured paradoxes.

Yeah, yeah,
he smacks me in the face
with a baby fist.

The yellow dog is in the green tree
the dogs are having a dog party!
that's what I meant

we are all on a smooth
green hump having a very
peculiar party in humid sky light

in suspenders and pantaloons
further description

always ends in its obliteration.

Madrid

appears to be a black oval.
enlarged, like twin giant keyholes.
The men at the bar watch the birds
through the tangibility of an awful sunlight

enormous historical place mats
amphitheater that encircles the rotating bull.

carve out of space with a body
of iron
that emerges from the stone in to the plaza
like a mouth
opens for the first expresso of the day

blue
covers the land
its prehistoric gesture a cold wool
skin
and architecture as background
to isolation.
Little burro, hungry horno
that rests on coral waves sleepily

the eye scatters its pictures over the wall
inserts rectangles of
"plumera rubia"
a leaf shaped like a canoe
pencil and watercolor on graph paper
of a moderne coffee set in 1928
which Josef Hoffman drew
sitting at a round table
in Madrid.

After "Turn"

for Mitch

The page was bronze
but weightless
in your eye
a wheel
invisible calculates
a direction
all around transcription's
tangible soundings
evidence of its primary substance
as you headed
North
a sight unseen requires nothing
but you gave everything to its beauty.

Abracadabra

We watch together
black collide with white.
This is not the night
falling around snow

or a mailbox swallowing
our letter
frozen dark air around ice cubes
the white sink cups
wet black pantyhose
like a lake seen
from the
small window of a train.

The window of a face
on film
big kosher salt in a small black pan.

One Hundred Famous Views of Edo

Tectonic

How the wheel becomes it
said Ophelia.
For it seems one
is called
or not.
Speech consists
of a short bar
with a metal bell.
A coulter is a cutting tool
used in assembly lines.
There are two alternatives;
holism, a constant shift
or programmed variety.
Ophelia,
is sound
the distance mounted?
I just remember
I dreamed
broken sound and
broken sight.

Duration

Moving at a fast velocity creates ascent. Beads of
atmosphere, a battle of registers and confused sound.
A substance parallel to the dark ahead.

Crossed lines, the branches of a tree seen looking upward
from the sidewalk in the middle of October in the late
afternoon. Apartment buildings of red brick. Count each one
to come upon the right number, the correct address. Undress
and lie on a bed in a room with alcove windows and stained
wooden floors. The bed is narrow and its short metal legs
rest on two telephone books. The doorknob is cut glass
and loose in the door. The porch projects from the wall like
a wooden ship. Once in the middle of the night there is a
tremendous thunderstorm and the flashes of light in the
room throw off the newly learned orientations. The
illuminations of wall, mirror and window open to another
shape to be memorized the way a bat sounds out the
densities and openings with wings and folds the image in.

When she opens the old cabinet built into the wall, the
drawer jumps out. Lined with yellow paper, it's filled with
sticky dishes, heavy tableware, an iron and disassembled
coffee pot. The aroma of the whole drawer is sour and yet
fascinating. She opens it many times even though they must
throw everything out, the whole drawer must be disposed of.

There is a corner where a chain link fence and a brick wall
meet. A line of bushes and tangled branches runs parallel
to the wall. The corner is roofed with the bushes and the
bricks are separated by an interesting yellow cement. She is
storing empty cans in the space made at the juncture of the
wall and the bushes. The feeling that she has about the place

cannot be recalled except when she goes there and stands
in the corner and thinks: this is it, this is that feeling.

Connected to the climb up the carpeted steps through
the hallway with brocaded patterned walls are stories mixed
up with a breathing hard that comes after a long walk
through other neighborhoods, a sensation of completion
that sparks an intense relief and simultaneous dread of the
process to begin once the door is shut and the life inside
begun.

Ice coated with powdery snow lines the streets and snow
clings to the sides of the building as though there has been
an explosion and white has stuck to everything. Her hands
crack and feel like they are under a tight film. It is hard to
know where one ever is or to be completely sure of the
stability and weight of things. They must be lifted and tested.

In the center of the town rises the temple. Strips of cotton
hang from the inside of the glass case over the reed chair.
Ocher pots broken into pieces are arranged around the head
of "woman, age 35." The folded bones, the blackened hands
crossed on linen. "Pretend you are a person in another period
of history. Describe how you might have lived and the foods
you might eat. Would you live as you do now. Explain the
differences."

Trays of tinfoil are held outside the airplane and raindrops
collected and counted. A plane takes off outside a hanger
at the end of a dirt road in the middle of a field of long
grass. The woods extend on either side. There are small lakes
with wooden rafts chained to the bottom that float on the
middle. Moss grows between logs and trees fall down when
your head goes in to the water under the lake to the mud
and the fish bursting from your eye.

A man sits on the porch with his back to the door, watching the dark in the back of the trees come forward. A sprinkler is suddenly cut off and there is silence. He finishes his drink and he gets up and goes and makes another in the kitchen. He turns on the light above the door of the porch. The woman with short blonde hair sits on the couch with the legs tucked under, reading a magazine next to a lamp. The girl is shaking uncontrollably in her bed and is covered with sweat. She cannot reach down and pull up the sheet because of the whispers and the criminals.

In the paneled basement they all sit together on a long vinyl couch and watch television. There are people laughing at the young brother's questions while his mother stands at a counter and mixes a cake. Above the couch there is a linen towel hung from a wooden rod. Stitched in red thread is a prayer in German. All day long they have been pretending to nurse children with polio. She trades off being a nurse, a mother and a polio child. The room grows unbearably hot but they cannot leave the babies to die alone on this hospital ward. They must reach them to walk and will carry them on their backs.

There are parking lots and cars frozen cold. They must get down to the store to buy anything. The leaves dry up and float down to the curb. They walk in packs, hurrying with hunched shoulders. She feels herself to be provisional, easily rubbed away by their bodies knocking into hers. She cannot remember what she looks like, even if she has a face. She is duct of words she repeats to herself to become a body. The body sits in a chair.

They go to an ice-skating rink and she discovers that she has no balance. No one will look at her absent face. They are wolves and she is a wolf too, she feels her forelegs move inside her pants. The river goes under a bridge between two towers, cans float on the water. They wait for a train on the platform and watch the lights come on in the cold sky. To explain this thing that is happening compels her to say something. When she gets there it has turned around and she has lost control again. The head is a lantern that swings, crashing into the air.

Lying on the couch, underpants stuck to her ass, the room is cloudy with cigarette smoke.

I am that man.

Her earrings are stone balls that cause pain. Her hair is short and the earrings give her head a balance. She looks ahead into the dark and feels the electric lights strung out over the stage to be the most joyous points of contact she has ever experienced. In a room with women and men she stands among them looking in to the long mirrors. She looks at the face which is supposed to be of a young girl in Wales. The town is waking up. The man is talking to the prostitute and the song he is making up to her bent back is about a cat and there are long tables with glasses of beer. No one notices her and she is dancing wedged in between them all. Then they go to sleep except for the man who watches from his window, looking down at the sea singing about his dead wife to no one in the room.

The distorted image of her body in the mirror makes the stomach look protuberant. They dance in the living room to James Brown and spill bourbon on the rug. The beating in her chest cuts off her breath. She can barely talk or answer his questions. He tries to answer for her and shows her some of the things he has in his jacket. They go to the lake and stand on the rocks next to the trees, and look down at the crashing gray water. She cannot see anymore. He tries to make her not shiver and says: damn girl, it's all right, stop shaking. She doesn't remember why she came here but every turn in the color of the water is because the light is changing it. He uses this to explain to her they must stay where men walk slowly along the edge of the rocks smoking cigarettes.

They rest on each other in the grass next to the wall. She moves her mouth on him experimentally. The black sky is between her eyelids. He moves in a circular grind on her pelvis. They are flat but turning over. She thinks a long sentence made up of pictures.

The woman is in the canoe, one hand in the water. A book lies on her lap. Just below the surface of the water is the body of another woman in a brocade dress, her hands crossed and her eyes looking up through the water at the sky. The boat is either going down or emerging. The woman holding the book is hypnotized, ready to say something she has said at another time and that erased fulfillment a force that has sent her into the water and the woman floating underneath the midpoint of her journey.

There is music to diagram. Every point is equally hard and the whole bunch of wands is assigned one tone. The streets are magnetic and thoughts change the way they look. The light bends at the window. The borders are the tall letters with small animals inside the curling lines. Travel through the suburbs to get to the city. Write in a diary but thoughts are transparent and hover over the writing hand.

Above the snow, Japanese lanterns. Mesmerized by synchronicity, there is an attraction to the other end of the story unseen at the beginning but certain as night.

They are one thing cut in two parts pulling from the center. No one hears his voice as he rides in his car through the Midwest. He counts the towns one must past to reach a point on the map by the hour he has been assigned.

She fits the landscape like a cap, finally making a body. She finds herself on the floor, her face to the basement and hears pins and wheels turn. She is sucked through the tunnel and floats above the rooms. The forehead, a pivot, turns around a cog. She opens the door. There is a gigantic auditorium filled with people. A massive wave washes over.

There is rain, curry, raita and lassi. Camels, he tells her, leave a single hair in each footprint in the sand. Saris are displayed on the mannequins and a radio and a toaster are also for sale. Breathe and let the air come from the stomach. Keep your arms at your side and the body will not tip over. The machines get louder and fill the night.

The train runs by the river. Birds mass together. The trees thin out and then the muddy river. The mountains fill up a hole that she has. You can hardly ever get away. Turn north and blue mountains. Green land and gold in the leaves. Winter chokes off the water and compacts a room. Outside the window, white stars and voices in the hallway.

She resolved to be like a point of a flame. The base is blue and the tip is white.

Memory is a machine. Cross a low bridge over rushing water around rocks. A woman with a blue shadowed dress with her hands extended at her sides in everlasting compassion. They eat doughnuts at the diner. She conquers herself and tries to analyze the parts. The long line of trees by the road and the white salty marks on the bark.

He walks through the woods at night and creaks the stalks with his legs. Lights are on in the houses and the water moves in the pipes. She feels controlled. It's the words linked together with prepositions that implicate the relationship. She can only connect to the part asking questions. The other part is like a campfire around a stump. She can put her hands in the ashes once the wood goes gray. They go over the river. The light finally fills the room. He remembers a story that he once heard about William Faulkner. They lie on the bed next to the white desk. An old woman coughs and a door shuts.

Inside the land there is a power that rises. The trees and the road between the trees. An animal crouches at the edge of the wood. The animal wakes her with fingers of blue leather on her eyes. Pumpkins lit with candles on the bridge. Everyone must go through the line of witches that stand over the river. The witches wear burlap dresses and plow the fields. The stone wall along the orchards and the apples fall on the grass. The radio is left on so long that it crackles with no voice and fills the car. A Dutch master and she a bowl of apples on his table. His hands are white and the apple is white under the skin. His afternoons are never filled but with singing and all variety of dance; the minuet, the waltz and delightful country two steps. The patrons kneel at the door bent over the book, weighing the gold on their scales.

In Peru, exogamy and infanticide. Matrilineal descent and potatoes on a high windy hill. At the market they sell blue stones and red cloth, carry huge puppets through the square. She tries to write the answers down. They talk about the problems but the anger is a shield and reflects hot light.

It rains on the road the triangle of grass fills with water. The parts of the self shift and collide. First she sees a luminous shape and then feels shriveled and human.

She goes around the dangers and they tell her: you avoid it, why can't you just say what you mean. But there is this gap, a ditch.

The city is a beacon and it is Rome filled with the partial heads and dishes of the long lost. The pink and gray marble and the coffee in the tiny cups. Gold frames and the flat Siennese faces. The muddy river she can hardly look at. Her skin flakes, her scalp crawls. A man hands her a bead. The walk in the garden around the cyprus trees and sloping banks. The dead babies have been removed but their name is Daniel and the red dress with the arms raised upward. A high ivory dome like a profound transparent skull. They talk too much, her boots are wrong, she cannot sleep, there is no explanation for this beauty, there is too much explanation. A man on the train in a white shirt and white pants leans against the wall and smokes a cigarette. The Museo has glass floors. The woman is partially is a tree and he desires her in order to stop that process. The cult of Mithrais in blue damp halls. The Christians took over the next floor. Bulls and lions and the contorted faces of the damned. The Etruscans faded and distinct at the same time. Olive oil drips on the bedspread and the water laps under the wooden windows. A prenatal dream floats oval between the door and the bureau. She is unable to plan a life in the face of this ornate intricacy that has asked every question.

In Florence, cold pizza under fluorescent lights. No one looks back at her. The mask breaks, the hotel elevator's wire cage. Jesus is blindfolded and carries a candy cane. The insane humor of these frescoes. The gold ring with the blue stone. The serpent is perpendicular to a track, the perspective divides the two sections joining hands over the closed doors of hell. People fall out and scream for a boat. Ursula in her red bed dreams the seven foot angel at the door.

The intertwining stories happen all at once. The purple, rose and blue walls and the spout from the door. The ice blue sky behind the orange faced virgin with her sketchy baby. The chairs like swan boats in this lake church. The hulk of rock rises from the water with stained walls. Erased scenes cut off by the sea.

The city is a graph of light. No sequences but coincidences of gestures. At Easter a barge down the river. Turn three times and go inside. Tell them they want you. Smoked eel, abalone, fried calamari. In the night there are no pictures, no memory.

She goes down under the water and holds her breath as long as she can. To let go of the air, to bring every stone on her back to the surface. Edges of the foamy water lined with buildings throw all the shadows forward into depth.

Shower

Today, Lauren, Lorna &
I crossed 2nd street
to view
the cemetery
where
Preserved Fish
lies &
saw a blue jay
eating a dead bird
really fast.
On the sidewalk
was a high heel
inside a suitcase
filled with rain.

Looking For Mina Loy

She was there almost
says someone about the long
trashy avenue with stores
for cups and plates.
Junky, glittery afternoons.
Fucked up high heels
and ashtray
with a hat of wings &
birds on it.
Piece of glass
a peculiar pleasure
as the windiness is
caving in. Your
red alphabet
in which roses grew backward
and come off the buckle.
Was it Athens or Aspen.
Someplace else white
and deep. The furniture
is ruined and beautiful
in the Bowery rain.

Ma Griffe

the opposite of everywhere
is this table
of chandeliers rusting
of roses protruding from a jar
to form a handle
made out of knives and forks
the ground shines
lightly and is a map
medicines in 100 miniature bottles
and green gloves dumped in a pile
of magazines about Barbie
and her lover Ken.
In my diary I wrote dear diary
today is 1957 and it's cold
today it was so cold
I could hardly walk.

Bright Blue

The eucalyptus
in the forties oval vase
the crystal goblet with wine to taste
this is the diameter
of Demeter
who points with her staff
ice dried, the river's wet
but we haven't silence from the north yet
I got my cards read last night by a guy with no touch
just a fireplace of cruddy candles
he warned me: falling tower, serene, then vandals
later, at Ed's
ate onions, cake, shrimps and bread
and read
a weird handmade Ted Berrigan book with kittens
chasing tanks through the demented pages written
while on pills I guess, why didn't I do that stuff
when I had time, too serious on one called the bluff
& now it's early to bed
a condition of eroticism
as I dance to Howling Wolf with red
underpants on
sometimes I wish I were blond
like my sister but it's out of date to henna
I've dreamed I had long hair looking in a mirror
with an antenna
which informs me of all within, hah, don't believe
that
I'm a kind of kinky brat
in disguise
as the mountains rise

suddenly too close to see
how the heavy curves deflect
the land of the text
pages of leaves internally fall
as references to times ago & to come are singing.

Rayographs

Statuettes and eggbeater
Chance outlives time
Framings combine
Occurrence in glass
Floats composition.

In his self portrait, a woman's hand.
Empty structure of white.
Though mediation
World which certitude
Make object.

In emotional contact
Fixed by light
Mind flowers fade
But permanent
The developing seconds
Excitedly examined.

Decided
and mysterious
Kiki.

A Fragment of A

Shall I fill a space
a chemise propelled by
an oarsman with a sweet flavored water
pulling alternately with the hands and legs
aim the beam
in the manner of a shepherd

dry to sweet shall I
remove a thin layer
from the weather
bleached white
as paper
rain
with a swift sideways
tremor

below as a water wheel
persons who yield no profit
tensely itching
United States Army
the unmodified species
thought to feed on the blood.

Aphra

A feeling that particles which were intended to represent
consciousness in an abstract field are germs, the dynamism
required to engender the organism. But that was the color
of multiple chemicals bonded into film. A frenzy of thoughts
rose as if on a platform towards a constructed sky where
there's all the sands he released from the frame. California,
a space of dry scents exemplified in stanzas, sections of
weather that disconnect from the main body and float
oddly at peace in such a sloping desert. Here is where my
eye touches other stones. Loose from the geology, each is
an interior of separated structures but risen, cling. The sun
moves horizontally through an abstraction of cactus, unlike
medicine or methodological but arrangement.

Anything bonds me except such purposes as I want to
receive. For instance, I admit I can't believe the thoughts of
these inter me: a new red satin bow. And the lamp, directly
electric. Cars line up, wait for possession. Metals grind then
leave anger as an explanation. I'm not so precision, do
demonstrate, leave myself remnants of blind signals. This
is the little chair hung in air, blue painted flowers on a fence.
But I don't want your intrusion. A kind of garden, more
a border of dirt where things appear haphazard. Then, a
feeling of night more than revision. A study of what remains.
A closet with metal trunk inside next to bags of plastic.
A hegemony one studies, a plan for dispersal, then
rearrangement. Patterns dissolve in a barricade of tensions.

Metropolitan inversions realign the nest of blackness.
This quarter reserves a strong light. Their longest river marks
the map in quadrants. Jumbled furniture, quartz chess board,
a lyre's shroud loosened the face of imperfections.

To listen to hymns exactly as they reach you. She expressed preferences for artichokes, holy dates. Played irreverently the lyrics on black webbed strings. A cheetah stands beside marble shoes. The vacancy of a room hides presence.

A lamp of hog fat fills this room with porky smoke. I'm on a cot, exhausted because of explaining. You're moody, once again cloudy and indifferent. I see your eyes on the horizon a magnet makes each axis singular. It's hard for me to explain how I make the earthquakes happen. Shards configure this astronomy. The ball rushes through its motions Titans hurtle bricks made of chemicals from one solar station. The hulk wears a cape of webbed rock. Trees rush through the seasons, loosing leaves like fleeing ninnies, then just a quickly reclothe and sit back comfortably to watch the sky turn light n' lovely for a day but stern and withdrawn the next. What do we care, we're just a bunch of dumb flowers drooping our big ears and sticking our tongues out at the bums.

Eventually I turn into a dwarf and crawl through the window. An old lady is setting out bowls of weed soup. She indicates with her hand the house is all circumference. One bed, a bible, and a glass of water. We lift barbells, watch TV, and do a little housework. She knows the McGinty's who live in a tree. There's a thirsty bee dipping in my yogurt but I swat it.

Oddly at peace, I go for a little walk. The hills are bumpy but I don't mind because I wear little slippers. Fortunately, it's sunny. I see an acorn as big as a house. I think I'm in paradise. I say: "this is a socialist country with a name like Zandra." Forty kids sing cocoon and hobble on their bikes. We count the blue ribbons, twirl on our bonnets. An engine starts up with the sound of a green siren. Who could care, the immersion of thinking a sort of blue and gold water that sparkles like linoleum. I come to a bar with a brat for a bartender. We make striped drinks in the blender. A kind of conical ice smeared with grenadine. I open a book with velvet pages. A prince met a quince and ate her.

When I remember you it's in pieces. Shirt with insignia, novels, chain saw, lock, pancakes, Ohio, districts. When is love not a constriction and so let the feelings. A zenith eclipses, antelopes gently mocking. In a quick dream you are at the back of a car. I pass you in a rainstorm. Now dark blue Navajo. Chrome. Feeling huge and undefined, partially an animal with hands to bring the soup to the mouth. Once the moon split into three, magically huge between trees. Cleaning the carpet gave tremendous relief. Picking lint cleared the mind of religion.

Scotland, scorched basilicas, anything plaid, brocade or red. There remain spaces when a day goes by just the way it looks: calendar, blank, girded in boxes. At night we wear raincoats and zip busy into rainstorms. Embers split off and make lightning. I like a carpet with Turkish squiggles, everyone's mouth shining. Luster they call it. The color of crystals with big pink shadows. And dots. Here is a dot to provoke your pencil. Please sign my perfunctory punctuation. We drink white coffee and marbleized chocolate. By now it's Wednesday, fur flies thickly. I can't thank you enough. Gold pediment pieces fall from buildings. Into my hand goes the referent. Thanks for that, hidden verb in my coat. These words turn envelope and mailed backwards. The rain moves up and down and looks like steel. To part the rain, turn in your chair. Smash the state. How did that happen, it won't happen again. Laboratory mice were early pets, Tigris and Euphrates. One did die eating a grape, a green grape and Mom did flush it. For relief, learn abstraction or

remembered retraction. Pointillism as a big hit because of
the gyration. A river drawn with blue ink and red fish. A flat
name, di ding or crossing.

But the climax a white quiet. Occult, lassitude, Jesus real
big up there dying. Somewhere in Spain a lance dripping.
Because of the epic wildness of the horses lighting splits
the sky in zones. The book changes to a record of families.
What I wanted was shadows which explicitly made skin out
of houses. The rooms with blue couches. Nipples on hands.
Through the balcony oceans and heart fills my head and the
heat fills the heart.

One Hundred Famous Views of Edo

The past
seems to leave a circular field
of sparkling braided messages
and red mud ditches in all the roads.
In the margins, a dry scratching,
poles around the dead blue thunder.
The centuries are poles and
the sky a procession
of configurations and tangents
rushing into depths.
Gestures, explosions
wrung dry, the animals pulse.
An undergrowth
of circular stubs,
powdery traces on the ceiling.
Loose sage piled in a glass,
the pageants are
blue bolts of silk.
Zones of talk
floating between us pack the sides in.

A mat of woven strands drapes this arrangement.
The horizon: lacy, rough
ice mountains and pines.
The idea of the eternal,
a stationary triangle,
the waves
around the ones who fish
for pearls for Leah.
Ash white flickerings of energy
become a new crust, a level
that rims the face

seen while tipping the head
out of the boat.
Looking for the book under water
Ophelia
clogged with speech
ricocheting off the appliances
in her brocade
abstractions and naming.
An ether floats off
the silo.

I always look for you
in that town, hope
to recognize your door maybe or the roof,
that weird old mansard.

In the tarot card two children meet
and exchange secrets, flowers and promises
against yellow buildings.
Who knows what "it" means.
Number Eleven. Fox hunt and harlequin.
Hurricanes, ice tea.
Horseflies
might take away your blood
on their wings, seem almost thoughtful
pausing on the white table
of our home in Kyoto.

In "One Hundred Famous Views of Edo,"
the umbrellas and snow bent figures
are far away, as they hurry to temples
while I hide in the doorway masked by
a paper lantern that's as huge
as earth is.

Future/past axis
conductor of thoughts
determining sets of
actions,
transparent shadows
on the rim of the virtual.

In detaching buds from the stems,
stacks of situations and enigmas.
Montage of chaotic, indeterminate surfaces
as the rain diffuses
the Empire State Building
which seems to float out of a cloud.
Trashed in the street,
all of the fascinating junk.
Gold and purple
tassels, three periwinkle glasses in the dirt.
Abandonment of a thing attached
gets worked out, right? A kind of
combing through of factors and tangents
so that the perspective
relays the context.
An entire structure of
relationship
but the pivotal
point in the depth
surrounded by dark rushing waves is
absent. Surrendered to,
a sensation of exactness
a wish to sing elegies
in another language, a ritual
hovered over in the old
magician's toy shop where
the rewards are sugary and elusive as
the snow falls outside the window.

The German town we got to just at dusk
approached through purplish towers of trees
and medieval houses built in 953,
the lit up windows of stores in the completely empty
    square.
Had a cigarette and a beer and listened to
opera through static on the radio
by the side of the road
while an undefinable panic set in.

To locate
the portal, the green
room with one light bulb and a cot.
Silverfish, fork and radio.
Outside Creech Funeral Home
in Middlesboro, Kentucky
wait for someone from
out of town to walk in and transpire
something to happen.

Miss Jane Bowles is joining us
for a Black Midnight cocktail
on the porch
with Miss Jean Rhys, in rhinestones.
Conjured materialized cloister's excursion.
A maze.

The paths, internal.

Object Relations

Object Relations

This summer I don't remember any paintings
did I just read the words "dry torches" or
think it
that seems to summarize the quandary

the quarry where several of us
roasted Episcopalian food in a funnel

dry wads
of lace from which spiders ran
in a tent packages of
buttons
that might be chips of tooth
or ivory
a cough that resembles the sounds of an old man

baggy, ridiculous orange shorts
grainy channels of air
grasshopper poised on clothesline
Japanese pin foil

in the autumn I ride a ferris wheel and
say the word cathect.

I don't like
her long pieces
they seem to
cut a lot of the
reader in the way
of connection

August

Trees fill
the window and
light
is thin, holds its dust.

On the bar
last night I saw
3 martinis,
trembling triangles.
Nancy said
this is the first time
I've felt happy.
Big white trucks.
I guess everybody goes there
at least once.

Sutured
is that kind of medical
worked.

August just whitens
things down.

Early moon between the two
most perfect black towers.
Gretchen has us notice.

Slowed down at the Dakota

and everything
looked hot, like a carpet.

White steam

poured and we just went
into it.

The alchemists invented
gin
as an accident, he said.

Central Park West

Summer sandals are worn down
lightning
flashes but
it's a jet
everything is so dry
rubs against everything

white shirt
on black file cabinet
when I hear air
it's the incidents in its wake

white blades of a fan
Twentieth Century French Poetry
"shock headed trees dripping moss"
lots of moss in France, I guess

now it smells cindery
drink iced earl grey
there are sirens
rain on the moon

depressed segment of earth

a soft black lustrous
source of pleasure
in the focal plane, granular high romance
imaginary syllable in which a dead person is
buried
recover sunken objects
study handwriting &
wound in healing.

The Hidden Staircase

Raw or dressed, behind
dark glasses
Male
Ceremonials
Clothing and bookbinding
To prevent straying
Collect in a hive & lymph nodes
Oh, small old world falcon
Take the horse nearest the door
Form high magnetic compounds
The American movie picture industry.
Sea cucumbers in crystal bonds.

Jeweled Fifties Bee

First you had the audacity
oh bird
bringing
some kind of
Braque broken
on book
with cup & saucer
and fried egg
boxing. A bee may
stutter and columns
abbreviate.
Light in to lamps,
cup around coffee
a hand distills
the petal the
stem threw away.

The Reginald Marsh Rose Couch
With Leopard Trim

in sleep a summoning
the 1940s hotel of baroque elevators
vaporous black and white spooky thorns
is Sharon's Egypt
thunder of
Grave's
biography reins blue egg for eyes
& tin shadow ventricles make the heart
fuck heart someone says this week but I forgot
be back shortly, baby.

Kind

In sleep the hubbub
of gestures.
Feeling pinned to a juncture
of undefinable objects.
Here it is all sheets of
color and the shadows
from the trees.
New leaves today
fall on the garbage cans &
cars look
stenciled on.
Surrounding orbit
sews together disparate
tones and edges,
fundamental nature,
quality or essence.

Moon, the Harshest Critic

Who combs her hair

a boat drags
leaves
into my mouth

"Chansons du Troubadours"
Trust, but don't
revise.

Ride
in his blue car, thumb the bible
napkins
Baltic's
that are glued
but when you pick up
a piece
the other piece falls too.

Wish to not be so conscious.
To come here to this park.
The earth becomes closer
yet turns away.

Vampyr

Coating
is the house,
a film
spook with thorns.

It comes down to the oldest woman in town,
the head locked into transparency
the spires.

This is the movies.
Phantom curtains the sick girl memorizes
how a man walks from his body
and becomes a wobbling emanation
that feels black
thread across the throat. Give me the bottle
named "x"
and shiny, silver field.
Boundaries on boundaries make the sickness
a cure.

Sugar, wheels and cog. The technology
of this town.
The machinery to mill
her will into bread.

From out of the black flowers.
a tincture.
Doctor, I'm calling from this forest
of spare, theatrical trees.

Marguerite
makes the syrup.
The head as a jar. Now,
with his book & net, he is all camera,
Porous film.

Infinite green
objects, their weird
functionalism.

Listen to my radio,
dry thunder.

The Teacup Club

> "Some copper of my things
> went all black and pieces"
> Laurie Price

Now the sky
is changed.
Changed

Like the tea
does
in a cup
drawing to the bottom
very light water
floats
as do

weird eastern clouds
at sunrise

I remember now
unwrapping out of purple
paper
gold shimmery
drops
I think from a dead woman's
hand
and shoes with palm trees
painted on.
I guess shoes are like cups,
in a way.

'Tude

Say "party hat," or "red couch," "lime
green popsicle," and "taxi." "Umbrella
tree," "indigo," "come," and "promise."
Breezy big snow drops, egg on the
head
from frying, it's so hot. Dinky white
carnivals
asleep in the river. What's that movie?
"Angels & Insects." Let's go to
The Somnambulist instead, talk about goofy
earrings
the dancers seem activated by our expectant gaze
or do they
project us.
Go in to the "powder room"
and comb your scrawny hairs.
Drink seaweed soup with stones in the broth.
I remember trying to make this
with Bridget MacNamara
in a driveway in the shadow of garages.
"Stone soup, stone soup" we chanted.
Old soldiers fall in to the river and
seals swim in murky, shiny,
clumps. The feeling of a nylon carpet
in a closet, the expectant white paper
inscribed with green wax.

Walnuts, shadows,
groves of tangerines. A glove,
perpendicular to the wind
absent of the hand
seems completely flesh

fills a person with shudders
a word a hair off from "shutters."
Black eye slips over the aperture
opens the swell box of an organ.
"Shudder" from old High German, to skutten.
Drink a coke in a diner
with a red ceiling
and trippy, sparkling linoleum
fills one with precipitant shivers.
Something scrapes
something from something
out of sight
as though all of life needs
to be portioned and moved, shoveled
from one pile to another.

And there's a big pile of it
covering a hydrangea bush.
Apricot streaked cream
papery kernels
wigging out in the sky
as it hypothetically descends
and is all around us now.

Oreos & Cheerios

After cookies &
milk in
pale blue winky bowls
we take a walk
past a factory (a cement factory).
A big black car slowly
is driven by. I think this was
jello, oreos, and cheerios, things
like that. Anyway, puffs
of round smoke are ejected
from the eye.
Then you see a house
with a bird and a key.
He's playing in the yard
and she's "coming over."
Every day is neutral, without
weather and people's heads
block the sun. People are
either scared or smirking.
You "go to the dance"
which has the same furniture
as the house.
Does your dad work at the factory?
He does two things: read a paper
and take away your allowance. Mom
wipes her hands on a towel
and yells down
the vacant street your name.

Your friends are
"at the dance" and they try
to trick you. Afterwards,
one special friend
pats your shoulder.
The only person you can
trust owns a
"soda fountain."

The sun protrudes
spiky hairs
above the soda fountain.
Things of life pass by

like on a conveyor belt.
Graduation "looms"
and you are in a bad mood.
Or sort of scared & smirking
when you trick your friends.

Gold autumnal strands
paint the buildings of the college
the colors of a fever.
Everything becomes complex,
ambivalent & dense.

Trudy gives back the ring.

You bury it in the yard.

It makes a big hump
by the bird and the sky.

Dad, I love the paisley
on the back
of your neck.

Mom stands with her vacuum
and stares a thousand years in to
the future. I guess the furniture
gets pretty dusty
inside its lines.
Buzz off that speck,
will ya.

College looms
like a paisley fever
a dance
of moods.

No one can adjust their
face or think
of a new thing.

A black car goes by
the factory
it makes cement.

March 6

Now it disperses
tentative

poking alone snow
drops

it is so gothic this morning
and foggy with debris
the strangeness

of random diffusion
and two lipsticks, black glassy

flowers on white shadowy
paper

and everything seems to be part of it
in the Japanese sense as Patricia said.

April

So frail its
like curtains or frill.
No one sleeps
late today. It
finally here
causing ferment or activity, yellowish
yoo-hoo & yoni.
Saw the word winch twice
today and a dry, thin stalk of grass.
Let's get drunk.

Ask Ivanna

What cool pipe dream
is contained in an asphalt
mound, parallel orange slats?

buried under pink tarp
bouquets, cellular ravines

my hair dripping south?

a soldier's house is
where? pu-leeze...

save the battlefields, huh?
at this stage the ceremony
is a mess, cremated sheets
of air the fragile, foggy
gloss on the lawn, blue
mountain muffins.

Advise, if you will,
the "sun lies on the land"
not really but sticks and
ivy that bear its brunt
feel it so.

Everything plus
the kitchen sink, you say?

plug up this depot at
Rockrimman
at the utterance of
white, star-shaped clusters
extrapolated from the
earth, oh girl
your fancies
an alternate route

and the light has pushed
against
its limits.

Universal, green, empty
how regalvanize
world shells

playland, good-bye.

Eon

There is the wobble of rain.
After the blue emanation,
soba noodles, bent daffodils and songs
emerge like a needle
from the windy fire,
cavalcade of horses and rocks.

In this anthem the moon
is a white fin that rigidifies in our iris
and hollow the mouth
that invokes, like a pump,
the five black stairs
to the ravine.

"Watchtowers of the North"
are compressed on the horizon
as those whitish trees between the Sonoco
sign and glaze of humidity
buckles the page.

I came to it with my mouth open,
half loaded.

The sonic dimension
was like this car that actually said:
"the door is ajar, the systems intact."

Now the goof balls will charge
the alabaster
tinges
and the classic will arise

cool as ice-cream
portable as the sun.

Sometimes it seems all of life
is this relentless machine
ordering you to its duty
but that's my excuse because I go
compliant as a maenad (Roman copy of a
Greek original)
head bent to the thyrsus
a mechanic with a flashlight.
All of the field is a warm
beige haven, a nothingness of particulars
punctuated by dinky Christmas tree lights
and the measured dance of transparent figures
around a glass vase
wedged in between a manila envelope
containing itself: the obstetric.

Women Working Wool (540 B.C.)
share this field
plaiting the strands of talk
tying off clusters
in geometric black dresses
in front of a weird, sunset colored space.
We go down to the Shohola
and the cool snakes
that inhabit the ledges
retreat slightly.

Immersed in its vault
night is spare, emits its messages
peripherally. How the rocks on the plank
feel as you pass by, wet as a dog,
remade by its fluorescence.

For instance: something happens.
The crack of rifles on the porch
as men in wool pants
aim their guns.

The divination wobbles then,
the ephemeral energies
of their traces
laid on the air and elm trees
gravitate to where hands hold the glass
and are asked the questions that have to be
asked.

How ever this room got made, the perspectives
rotate
so as each wall is a universe
of ordering nodes
and a cat will chase a snake will bite the bee
in days to come watch and see.

It was a place rumored to be a cairn,
some kind of underground bunker bar
in which out of work guys hunker down
and all of the textures are off kilter
and damp. The curtains
are printed with miniature spuds and elks
that chase the bride down the hill
into a minty vale
and a mighty blue nighttime.
But when we drove up
the neon hissed through the rain.
A man who had met the pope the day before
tried to sell us his grandfather clock.
Later, I took that as some kind of indication
that time is cultural,

organized along corporate lines
chopped up any old way that serves the
dominant ideology, dressed
in clogs, nails and
bandages, the transparent linen
threads loosely folded to resemble
hair
but peering through the rags at the portal
there was only the ancient slime beloved
to its manufacturers and useful as a
lubricant.

A whirling vortex of fragmented conversations
threw of sparks
shards of the beautiful shale
that banks the old road
all of the big wet leaves,
triangular blades, lie on the pavement
as though positioned by the black figures
working wool

to be read as a copious text
reverberating echoes
off of the other centuries and
written to keep us
writing the next.

If you break an alphabet
and place it in a circle
let Eon choose
its reconfigurations
the long sentence out of the mouth
the mouth of the universe all
projectile, sequence and charms
that vibrate multidimensionally.

The currents
a magician's
punctuation.

Okay, some take mystification
and make it magic.
Like the fluid shape of
an enormous body
enclosing the Shohola's detritus
the water
holds her as she passes underneath us,
a mirror that
contains negation and desperation.
Eon's breath on our hands
scrambles the cubes
and makes new words as the old alphabet,
syllables of identity, erode in the flicker
of a fire that lines the path.

I stood by a funny
old bedroom lamp of brown paper
and green ceramic horses
examining the latch on a red purse
when you came in. We talked about
the perimeters
that seemed to
be as transparent as dragonfly wings
and just as tactile and expansive
but there was also this sense
of a vocabulary diminishing
around the core of feeling
that generates
this molecular vibrancy.

I sat on the bed
picking at white chenille
while the letters hilariously run away

because as the night comes on
even the furniture slopes
and there's a multiplicity of objects.
There's too much of everything,
more than the amount with which we started.

Our love
becomes a sweeping plum
atmosphere
elements attend.

This exhaustion
elastic and stable
yields recognition
of narrow, billowing shapes,
electrical snaps
along the line
as you approach
discernible entities,
monstrous, beloved
manifestations.

At the instant
of equivalence,
the radio starts up with that
haunting music from Afghanistan, love duets.
The clock seems literally to
wring the hours dry and
screws them back
on to the ramp

and we have many things to tell you
of the flood,
the low-ceilinged room with gun racks
and a string hanging from the ceiling
and a daddy longlegs
walking on the rim of the toilet.
The photograph of twelve dead deer
lined up for a portrait on the snow.
There is a continual crackling that comes
from the woods in the morning
and later you realize it's the sky that scratches
their name, the Lanape, indecipherable
as a stem that's lost most of the leaf
but they are buried in the ground out there.
She sleeps under a painting of two women
who sit in chairs
in ornate lace gowns, an artery of blood
ties them together like a clothes line in the
back yard wind.

Although this is a specialized space
that ties us to the twins
as if it was a wholeness
a way of keeping in sight everything
all of the edges as you focus
on the middle as
the sorting process begins
chambered until the day
its innate spectral beatitude
and lamentation flows through us.

Inside a circle of glasses
from the bodega, white candles.
To articulate the effect
of a motion just passed through as
receding frames of the thresholds,
you feel freaky
encapsulated in cognition and substance
inside the great, driving lucidity.

To move around and situate
is just so many lost repetitions, a dry mouthed
ballet against irreducible solids.
Finally, you let yourself
be put aside gradually
as a partition. The content
held in the body
as provisional a filter as that is.

A web, a curtain
of filaments
how the matching motions of the
other partially seen
sequences the chain.

Nothing might jerk the other side
just as likely
but since the jug rounds
you never do see
all of its content at one time.

I ride in his black car,
thumb the bible
tonight's not like
other nights; we
play charades w/
the moon
fuck on the leather
by mistake—
    one easily undone
"mon coeur, je t'aime

About the author

Kimberly Lyons was born
in 1958 in Tucson, Arizona.
She lived in five states of
the union before her family
settled in Chicago, Illinois.
Lyons graduated from
Bard College in 1981.
A psychiatric social worker,
she now lives in Brooklyn
with her husband Mitch
Highfill and their son
Jackson. She is the author of
several chapbooks including
*Hemisphere's Planetarium
Petals* (Situations, 1999),
Rhyme the Lake (Leave
Books, 1994), *In Padua* (St.
Lazaire, 1991), a fourteen
poem broadside *Oxygen*
(Northern Lights/Brooklyn
Series, 1991), *Strategies*
(Prospect Books, 1983),
and *6 Poems* (Lines, 1982).
Mettle, a thirty-six part
poem illustrated by Ed
Epping, was published by
Granary Books in 1996.